Red Lanterns

Red Lanterns

Poems

Janisse Ray

Iris Press
Oak Ridge, Tennessee

Cover Art: Raven Waters
Book and Cover Design: Robert B. Cumming, Jr.

Iris Press • www.irisbooks.com

Library of Congress Cataloging-in-Publication Data

Names: Ray, Janisse, 1962- author.
Title: Red lanterns : poems / Janisse Ray.
Description: Oak Ridge, Tennessee : Iris Press, [2021] | Summary: "*Red Lanterns* is a collection of new poetry that navigates a borderland between the seen world and the spirit world. Occupying a tangible world is expected of us humans. We have been taught to trust (and trust only) our five major senses, which inform the tangible. Humans, however, possess senses beyond our primary ones, not simply the sixth sense of intuition but also a sense of time, sense of responsibility, sense of being watched, and so on. Some things lie beyond the realm of human knowledge, some things are not as they appear, some places that appear empty may not be, and some things remain wild, secret, and intangible. These poems look at the place where the wild and mysterious joins with the explicable. The poems are about connections, especially spiritual connections—human to human, human to animal, human to land, animal to animal. Many of the poems can be classified as love poems, because love is one of our most primal connections. There is also a thread of fierceness that runs through this work. This ferocity is in seeing disconnection and fighting to restore connectivity. More than anything the book is a manifesto to protect all the connections that allow us to be creatures of spirit as much as creatures of what Flannery O'Connor called 'weight and extension,' meaning of the body." — Provided by publisher.
Identifiers: LCCN 2021002291 (print) | LCCN 2021002292 (ebook) | ISBN 9781604542592 (paperback) | ISBN 9781604548150 (ebook)
Subjects: LCGFT: Poetry.
Classification: LCC PS3618.A9824 R43 2021 (print) | LCC PS3618.A9824 (ebook) | DDC 811/.6—dc23
LC record available at https://lccn.loc.gov/2021002291
LC ebook record available at https://lccn.loc.gov/2021002292

Acknowledgments

"Eve of St. Valentine." *Yalobusha Review.* 2004.

"Mr. Coal." In *We All Live Downstream: Writings about Mountaintop Removal,* edited by Jason Howard. Louisville, Kentucky: Motes Books, 2009.

"One Fine Day in Illinois." *Notes from the Dells:* Newsletter, Severson Dells Nature Center. April 2015.

"Rant, WonderFarm," published as "Rant Delivered at WonderFarm, June 6, 2015." *About Place Journal,* Issue "South," edited by Ann Fisher-Wirth. May 2017.

"Red Lanterns." *Flycatcher Journal.* January 2012.

"Sicklefin Redhorse." In *A Literary Field Guide to Southern Appalachia,* edited by Rose McLarney and Laura-Gray Street. Athens: University of Georgia Press, 2019.

For Daniel and Ellen Corrie

and with gratitude for the work
of Robert B. Cumming, Sr.

Contents

iv.

v.

i.

Red Lanterns

1.

After the burned station in Jesup the train
crossed the Altamaha where bream inscribed
circles on gray water, past box houses, past
a man patting a softball before he lobbed it
toward his son. I sped toward Philadelphia,
past young trees like elephants with no elders:
surely they wonder how many years are left.
I know that even the trees are afraid.
Trees are the earth's lungs.

This week my mother lost her right top lobe
to cancer, four-inch scar under shoulder blade.
What we humans are doing to the earth is a
lobectomy, reaching beneath ribs, ripping out.
How much time is left?

2.

Meanwhile, my son's stepmother called
to say she found something strange
under the bed of my son, young man
tall and beautiful, head of wild black curls:
A jar packed with the blossoms of poppies.
Imagine summer sun on his dark head bent
in a flower garden, gathering red lanterns.
What would I rather him do?

3.

The berries of poke make ink.
The ashes of oak make lye.
The backs of certain toads
make you hallucinate, if you lick them.
Wormwood distills into absinthe.
Vitamin C in white pine will
keep you alive on a long journey.
Mushrooms can kill you.

4.

My mother was burning up, skin welting, reaction
to medicine, distillation of morphine. With a wet
cloth I swabbed her, day and night in a hospital room,
view of a roof, dark thunder-cloud, distant trees.
I didn't do anything to deserve this, she said.
Sky darkened, sky lightened, sky dilated.

5.

Some years ago I began a study of death,
how to take care of the dying,
how to die well, final wishes, last words,
then what remains: gardens of poppies.
I didn't invent the madness of this world.
I've tried to change it, for my son if no one else,
he whom I've ruined for industrialization.

6.

When I called to tell him his grandmother
made it through surgery, they think
they got it all, she's resting, she's fine,
he was at the river, swimming in a silver pool
where boulders are large and the river wide
enough the sun reaches in, between tall trees.
That is the place, I remembered, I tore leaves
from wild lettuce, to soak its sticky white resin
onto mints. They help you sleep.
Even swimming I'm thinking about her, he said.

7.

Something, of course, has to fill
the hole in my mother's breast
where a lung should be. That clearcut.
What to place there—
a clear jar filled with poppies.

Eve of St. Valentine

Weeks of unusual winds.
A pine struck by lightning
leaning toward evening.
The day my husband cradled
sapling longleafs in the field.
The day my father drew a line
between me and him.
A line always there.
Imaginary.
I looked at him and crossed it.
Crossed it, crossed it,
line of old tree,
lightning line.
It's down.
Oh, stop your blowing, wind,
now the tree's down.

All of the old trees leaning
one way or another.
Sudden red bloom of cardinal
in the dooryard quince.
Winter sun flaring on its breast.
My father carrying his wounded heart
in its cradle of ribs
out the old door.
The compressed. Slanted.
Blown over.
I wish I had a hand so strong
it could straighten damaged things.

The tree beginning to fall
and no one hearing.
Voice of wind

steadily urging it down.
Dough rising in the kitchen
over a pan of fresh-boiled water.
My father walking out
along his old fence line,
heart line, lightning line.
Not imaginary.
The pine green and strange
on the ground.

I like to imagine
in the wordless space of falling,
a cardinal in pine branches
like a winged red heart
flew free of the crashing ribs
of limbs.

Years After He Went to Live with His Father

for Silas

At summer's end the corn is tall, studded with plump ears,
and beyond the green rows, across somebody's farm,
the Connecticut River shines. How did I last those years?
Part of grief is for what I missed—when my son ran through
corn mazes, searching for an exit, turning ever toward
a great and distant love—and part of grief is for what
absence comes to know. Now he drives me along the river
past farms with bales of fresh hay and luminous barns
wherein horses and cows stand and wait.
He is tall and strong: he is driving me, his mother.
The corn waves long pennants, raising a rustle like a voice
that carries along the fields to the river, emptying.
Yesterday in a shop he showed me a book of photographs,
mothers and sons. In one, a man held his frail bird-mother
on his lap, anonymous aged woman and son now grown
beyond anything she imagined. Here is our portrait:
My son is driving. The corn is tall, heavy with sweetness.
Below, the unhurried river is shining.

ii.

One Fine Day in Illinois

It was spring.
Our canoe pressed
the crinkling silver of
Kishwaukee's South Fork,
against a stiff wind
hinting of storms,
through orchestras
of chorus frogs,
clatter of a kingfisher
startled over and over,
flurries of warblers and swallows.
We shoved onto a muddy bar
and entered on foot
a grove whose buds guarded
their memory of snow.
It was the time
of bluebells' blooming.
In the forest,
underneath leafless trees
as far as we could see,
the wildflowers,
knee-high, leaves tender
in the greening, turned
their faces toward the light,
their brightness like a ringing,
the small blue bells
clear and jubilant—
voices of our ancestors,
voices of all we've lost
and seek to recover.
We sat on a wet log
in the middle of
ghostly blue singing.

One among us
said he thought
when we died
we'd be given jobs.
Someone with a tiny brush
will paint bluebells blue.
Someone with a bigger brush
will tint the sky.
Someone will sprinkle glitter
on the Kishwaukee.
Someone will stack river sticks
so the gold goose can build
her nest above flowing waters.
Someone will crown the kinglets.
I will gather flowers
from their place
along the South Fork
and bring them to you.

Instruction

The children have gone into the old trees,
and the young trees have closed behind.

The children are gone a long time, playing.
When they return, cheeks flushed, eyes

bright as pieces of sky, they are more solid.
They are taller. They more easily bend.

Words come out of their mouths like birds.

Sentencing the Heron

for Rick

What crime did a heron ever commit?
Except trespassing in swamp,
among duck-potato and wild rice,
taking what belonged to the otter.
Coveting what she did not possess,
for example the great open flower of sky.
Speaking out in harp and trumpet.
Staying silent when expected to speak.
Fording night to navigate the perfect temper
of tides, scoring mudflats with graffiti.
Befriending the transparency of noon.
Admiring another's fog-blue plumage
mirrored in water.
Exhibiting wantonness.
Loving indiscriminately.
Loving freely.
Or fleeing a scene, sailing high and easy
up the mid-courses of American rivers,
claiming all tributaries as her own.
Craving distance. Demanding solitude.
Worshipping false gods of the marsh.
Building altars of pearl snail shells
and dainty carcasses of sunfish.
Offering piety to the alligator,
exonerating the water snake.
Not believing in numbers.
Keeping company
with the moon.

Bald Point, Florida

The business
of the oak snake
is to know where
goldfinch feed.
Cloud business
is keeping Orion
covered.
The hummingbird's
business is to
investigate red,
while the flower
deals in turning.
Our business
is not to take
this ardor
for granted.

Wilderness

Deep in the wildness
I feed sticks to a campfire—
a sun's glowing consul.

All day long
I feed that campfire
like a child.

All day, one
bird calls the kingdom's
longest song.

Counting trees
gives them a number
they resist.

Near dark, only you
and a bird are shocked to discern
the nature of our remove.

What I Would Tell at Confession

Something said *Look left.*

I was driving, thinking about a doe near Paradise
that ran out in a wrinkle of highway, how
a stranger helped to ease her from the road.
I had cupped her belly, white and heavy
as the moon, warm, workable as dough.
Could be she's fat from spring, he said.
I gently squeezed from her dead nipples
beads of colostrum, viscous and clear,
and put my finger to my tongue.

Now I looked left.

A flat meadow stretched away,
redolent with wildflowers—long-plumed
avens, bluebells, and cranesbill.
A creek ran through the meadow
and in it a moose stood browsing.
Her coat was rich chestnut,
gleaming wildly, as if she'd newly risen
from the forge of the earth
and stood cooling in the creek.
When she lifted her head,
cress dangled from her mouth.

Nothing came between her and fire.
Nothing came between her and loss.
Nothing came between her and nothing.

Three Wishes

The first: not to fly but to run like water.
Faster. Like wind, ground peeling from shoes.
The continent of Australia a day-long blur
so as to know it abstractly.
Kangaroos falling away like brown dashes.
A particular sunshine only rushing wind inhabits.
Panning the country.
To see nothing but everything.

Two: to see everything.
Especially spirit. Prophecies,
destiny, magic, the unreal.
The body an afterthought.
So the man who photographed children
with cancer can show us God weaving
among idling cars on his bicycle,
streetcorner drunks waiting for release.

The third wish: to not look back.
To run so fast the limits of flesh are broken.
Breaking free of the world.
Not death. Not now.
But merging. Stepping off land's edge
the way a migrating warber
blends into the omniscient sky.

200 Years after Lewis and Clark

If this is the last day of the world
I do not want to die here,
not with the bison gone,

and black-tailed prairie dogs in their towns
along the Missouri, gone, like mountain plovers
that nest-scraped in the grass.

Miles into the Elkhorns,
the thunderous purple of larkspur drenches the aspen
meadows along Eagle Creek

and mountain bluebirds lay eggs in a mud-cup
dried to lichen-green,
borrowed from the swallows.

On the way from Townsend today,
on a steep, rocky grade,
my tire caught a garter snake—

slender, eyes of quicksilver,
body dusted with charcoal and sulfur.
That quick he was dead.

When I picked him up,
something snapped, recoiling around my finger,
a bullion hitch tightened down.

It was punishment enough.

iii.

Huntress

In the art museum
        nude Diana restrains her hunting dog
            who would tear from her
                the way the sun leaps
across the ledge of the world
        each morning
                out of dark woods, following
                    trails of day.
The dog is eager for deer,
        for unwinding a bronze scent
            until it is under foot
                and in the jaws.
Hand on its collar, Diana
        braces, her knees bent, her arm outflung,
            her dog lust-driven,
                almost unrestrained.
My heart is like the hound.
        It would go leaping
            through sedge
                where you have passed,
lunging toward the orange possibility
        of igniting
            one irrefutable fire
                threading dry grass.
When is the moment
        Diana sets the dog free?

I See You as Raptor

Praise the harrier.
His wondrous eyes compass a low hill.
His white underbelly offers itself.
His wings are fluent with air's inconstancy.
He knows ecstasy, part of each flight nothing but joy.
He turns and folds his weapon of beak.
All sin is pardoned before he drops,
deadly sun-struck sickle cutting
blue sky above a yellow field.

Driving with the Beekeeper down Old Miccosukee

Somewhere within its green vines,
the kudzu has a G-spot.
The long tongue of road goes looking
for it, parting verdancy,
lapping among wild rustling leaves
that embrace whole hillsides,
tightening around erect trees.
The kudzu is blooming
erotic purple bliss.
It smells like Nehi grape
and drives the bees crazy.
We hear them buzzing and whirring
their excited wings.
For miles and miles
while the afternoon trembles
the road will not stop looking,
sliding its splendid finger
between her green curves.
Above, the beautiful legs of live oak
lock into canopy.
We overhear two bees talking,
somewhat breathlessly—
Wait, just you wait.
Watch what happens when he finds it.

When You Kiss Me

A herd of horses come galloping up the road
to the river, through Moody Swamp,
led by a mare the color of split cedar,

through the tall cypress and chestnut oak,
as if thunder broke from ancient-bark trees
or from the water-stained ground.

When they reach the bar at the landing
they paw and plunge, whickering.
Their feldspar hooves drive blown sand skyward.

The copper mare enters the river first,
ash-dark water sucking and pulling her
toward a mineral channel centuries deep.

In flanks the horses storm the river,
until the spray is full of them
as a breast is full. They are chaotic and beautiful.

Ragged, breath torn, the river goes giddy.
Light polishes its waves to silver.
Behind, the swamp moans a dark eternal.

A wind rushes to tie its invisible ribbons
among the heads of swimming horses.
When you lift your head,

the lead mare clambers up the far bank,
pausing before she leaps through a green thicket.
The herd follows,

undulating ridges of roan and bay a bluff
risen from the trembling river,
disappearing into woods.

The Last Hours

Two bodies softly press,
from one margin to the end.
They say something about softness.

Meanwhile, snow clouds breath deep
over the valley. Snow falls
mute against the ground.

Snow falling at night
makes a private room.
Nothing is quieter.

The couple sleep among
blankets and pillows.
Theirs is a world they don't understand.

Sleeping, they dream *tiger.*
Canyon. Lotus. Crucifix.
Also *hush.*

When they wake, the man says,
Tell me about the sunrise.
Rent in indigo sky, she says.

The night was not long enough.
Yellow advances steadily
toward its blinding brilliance.

On the street people are walking.
Church bells hardly stop ringing
before a priest will lift his hands.

Nickel-colored snow limns
the trees like blooms.
A crooked line of geese flies over.

When sun leaps through long windows,
the woman bursts into tears.
The snow is sliding into water.

From all around comes
the loudness of dripping.

Guitar Bound to Silence

Every room where you have been says no.
Books lean coolly on their shelves.
Knights and pawns on a marble board
stay silent, although they saw
your elegant hands and the disks
of your lambent eyes.
They saw the tender anvil of your chest,
your arms sturdy as cordwood.
The last of the kindling you chopped
started this morning's fire, and
within days even motes of skin
that drifted from your body will vanish.
Oak table where you sat, lamp that lit
your face, window through which a pale
yellow moon set sail: All say no.
The tea cups sit quiet and empty.

Hollow, the Bittern's Bones

My heart is a culvert, uninhabitable.
Your letters blow like wastepaper
through bitter-cold streets.
Sometimes in the marsh the bittern
freezes so still, head skyward,
she's mistaken for reeds.
Every bone in her body's a reed's bone,
her heart nothing but a flamboyant reed.
The stripped leaves of your letters
rattle against each other.
Once I saw a house burn,
flames reaching for the sky
until the walls came crashing down.
Months later an old man combed
the rubble for a wattled cup, a sooty coin.
When the bittern calls at evening
she sounds like a hydraulic jack.
Something happens in the translation.
Last night I dreamed you showed me
not a tree but a picture of a tree,
leaves yellow-red and dropping.
Now wind hammering the reeds
makes me think a bittern is there.

Postcard from Lake Patzcuaro

Dear friend, nothing I can say in this postcard
will be sufficient to reclaim the thing lost between us.
Tell me what is not tender, fragile, ephemeral?
So much happens by accident or without consent.
Nothing lasts. In the rubble of the island's lee,
away from other tourists, high above the lake,
I find fragments of pottery, the handle of a mug.
Orange-flowered mint grows determined
in the midden. A child begs for a peso.
Dearest, my friend, old love, though nothing has
turned out as we thought, what remains is recognizable,
thus slanted, indomitably and despite all odds,
toward love.

Mineral Bedrock

O shining trout, shimmering river, tallgrass netthrower,
will you remember me when arrowleaf balsamroot
turns the meadow yellow? Will you look deep into the eyes
of pines and remember the world we briefly knew?
Will you say, *There was once a woman?*

O wooden boat, blue-feathered flautist, coyote,
when lightning tears open nightsky, will you say,
I knew a woman who dropped like rain, season brief as lupines?
We were a comet that did not return.

Every day another world drops off the back of the universe.
Every day something precious goes up in flames.
Every day something with wings falls.

O tired dreamer, testimony of tongues, thunderbolt,
will you tell of that place far from here
made mostly of trance, beautiful but uninhabitable,
a long time ago?

iv.

Funeral

for Milton

During the service a tufted titmouse was calling
and, farther off, a purple martin.
I didn't learn enough from you.
Not the best student, I.
I was more interested in delight than names.
I still reference field guides to know turkey vulture from black.

From the hole dug for you, I carried home a rock.
I carried a bag of the earth, sandy, orange as a towhee breast.
Sandhill cranes passed, strange mournful trumpets.
Maple samaras flushed the lowlands.
Afterward I walked your farm,
through clouds of Chickasaw plum blooms,
their perfume one sweet room under a big heaven.
Each miniature goblet offered a few drops of nectar.

More and more I understand ecstasy as small wonders.
I understand myth as the chance to love at all.
Everything must finally be surrendered.

Someone had to identify the titmouse for me.
My irreplaceable, I wanted to hear you say it.

The Death of Mister G

I'll start with the day we met,
feeling as if I'd arrived for an interview.
The sick-room no office,
deathbed I saw
through an open doorway.

I came because death is mystery,
one of the last left,
or because among books, papers,
semaphores, I yearned,
so that perhaps my need
drove me to you whom
I could not help.

You were at the door asking
me to come in—*come in
and sit down and
tell me about yourself.*

That's how we started, how
the hours passed, three of them,
you in your chair by the window,
never wanting to go outside, not
liking it for whatever reason,
me in my chair on the other side
of the lamp, us talking.

I had come to a place where
my life was unwinding
and I missed everybody who had come
and gone.
Mostly I missed Milton, old friend.

So I went also
because that day in the pine trees
when he went down, torch
in hand, I was so far away
I could not have arrived
in time had anyone thought to call.
I wonder if my presence could
have thickened his blood,
coagulated his life.
When I heard, I ran
through the house hysterical.
I have never felt
like that.

But you were not my Milton.
You were not a farmer,
you made fun of hill farmers.
All your life you ran a store downtown,
all your life commerce,
a businessman, all business.
I might as well be a secretary
come to read the mail except
you knew better than anyone
the time for secretaries
was over.

Do you watch birds? I asked.
No.
Do you have a garden?
No.
Do you walk the woods?
Do you collect bird eggs?
Do you pick up deer antlers?
Do you make wild plum jelly?
Do you grow roses?
Do you build bird houses?
Do you laugh?

There was *one* commonality: books.
You piddled with pen and papers.

I could have been assigned
anybody. But you, wanting
your wife to golf
over the summer, told them
you liked to write. It may be
nothing, coincidence.

The day I remember most is one
when in the quiet apartment,
no television, no music,
a neighbor coming home
shopping bags in hand,
one of many silences,
out of which you said, *What*
do you think happens when
we die? And after a moment,
me thinking, This is the conversation
they trained us for, what did they
tell us? I said,
I don't know,
which is the truth.
But what do you think?
I don't believe in hell,
I said. *Probably not heaven.*
Okay, I'll be honest.
No heaven. No God.
And you said then, *If you*
are right, then millions of
priests and ministers and rabbis
are wrong.

Another difference was that
Milton didn't think I was wrong.

Never once did I dread
going to sit in silence,
every Monday morning
while Mary golfed.
Sunflowers in hand, chocolates,
books, kale, I knocked eagerly.

Those weeks, I saw more of you
than your own children.

When I arrived, you left off
your writing and your
pretense of writing
and we began our ritual
of sitting, businessman
at the end of his life
and younger woman who
could be his secretary, his
assistant, his coach, his
writing teacher.

You who never published,
who could have published,
who wished for another life
to start again, except this time
start writing earlier, with
more seriousness.

When I departed, true
to the image in your head:
man of decorum,
hard worker, son who made
something of himself,
you returned to the
desk, that endless
motivation that kept you getting
out of bed, even on the morning

50

of the day you died.
You didn't want the part about
laying while family
and friends sat vigil
holding your hand, standing
looking down. Rubbing
your feet was
out of the question.
No proper businessman
would have his secretary
rub his feet.
At the end, you simply
sat at the desk, unwilling
to forfeit.

On the road to Pisgah
on our way to Spofford Lake,
to see the lilies at the lake house
before it sold, that one day,
there was a doe and a fawn, standing.
They did not spook.
We eased toward them in the quiet car until
they could see us blinking.
They dove into a green cove of trees.
The lilies were blooming.
You were saying goodbye.
You were saying goodbye to everything
you'd ever known, to all
you'd loved and not loved.
When I die, I'll miss lilies too.

As I left for Europe, short
vacation, you told my husband:
Make sure you get her back.
And I, *Make sure*

you're here
when I get back.
The day before we left
you rang the doorbell, wobbly
on your cane, with a book
of French phrases.
Now go study, you said.

Something felt wrong
through Holland and France.
Two weeks is not time enough to die.
A Friday morning as I
embarked for home,
flying from Amsterdam
out over wild Greenland,
then down the Atlantic coast,
almost exactly the time we began
our journey,
you began your great journey.

You were breathing slow, then
rattling, then a nurse called the family
from the hallway to come,
you had crossed once,
it wouldn't be long.
Then you crossed for good.
Something, nothing.

The daughter told me
that you tried to wait but
I think she was wrong.
You tried not to wait.

Ode to Joy

In Memory of Troy Davis
Oct. 9, 1968–Sept. 21, 2011

The man inside the prison minds the approaching hour. Whether he is guilty or not, I don't know or care. I could have traveled on, but I saw the sign for Jackson just as the radio reported protestors gathering. I am Troy Davis, people. I am Troy Davis. Let me follow the coroners to Jackson where at 7 p.m. I am supposed to be executed for killing a man, a police officer in Savannah, or for someone else killing him. The protestors are a blood clot at the prison gates, as close as the cops allow. A military helicopter circles over ranks of police in riot gear. The crowd breath is chant and prayer, but, underneath, pulses beat with anger and with outrage. I am Troy Davis while Troy Davis sits wearing his scholarly glasses, minding his breath and his pulse as his spool runs out. He is calm; he is praying.

Now at the front line, up against the police tape that keeps us off the highway, I'm eye to eye with a line of officers. A young angry black man is beside me, another on my other side. These are my brothers, people, and I am Troy Davis. My time is running out unless you can hear me, Lord. My hour cometh. As it cometh, a drumbeat roars. This could be a war, us versus the Jackson State Penitentiary, where, somewhere within, Troy's sister spends her last moments with her brother, she who worked so hard for new evidence to be considered, who perhaps was the best person of all to judge Troy's innocence, which is my innocence, and later—I can hardly bear to think of it—how arduous will be her journey. Somebody needs to write about this night in Georgia, for it's night now, and nobody's leaving, just more coming. People are kneeling in the grass; people are stamping and chanting, "Free Troy Davis."

The stars are coming out, but they're hard to see with all the prison lights and the crowd pressing. It's 6:30 now—it's 6:30, people. The whole world is watching what we do tonight to a young black man in Georgia. When the word comes to break the line, I break it. What do I have to lose? But the police are on us like flies and—no surprise—they tackle the black man to my left, four white officers on one man. How do we think we'll last? They are at my feet wrestling him down and handcuffing him, with the terrifying clock always ticking. When he is an old man, I ask it, will he tell his grandchildren how he got arrested the night they killed Troy Davis?

Somebody has told Troy we are out here at the gates praying and chanting but mostly praying. Waiting inside ever so far away, Troy imagines he hears us.

Suddenly word comes of a stay. There's the stay we wanted. I can be on my way where I was going, but I don't leave yet. A church down the street has been open all evening for bathrooms and water—it's a black church—and I make my way through protestors and chains of cars and buses and signs, and I enter a sanctuary where a choir is singing, singing so hard I've no doubt they could lift the church off its foundations. This choir could beat down walls. They are lofting nighthawks into a dark sky above Jackson, Georgia. They are causing trees to bend, they are moving mountains, fruit is falling. They won't stop singing, even with a stay.

A few hours later I am not there when word comes that Troy Davis is dead—short stay, trick stay. I am Troy Davis, people, and my soul goes sailing into the dark night above Jackson, out over the people left clinging to the flanks of roads, over the church with its doors flung wide and its roof cracked open to the stars.

Miscarriage

The secret is out,
waiting to be buried
on Waterworks Hill,
Salish burial ground,
to become
as much a story
as anyone up there.

One evening this week
a man and woman,
hearts crossed,
leaking, will part
strands of barbed wire
under a No Trespassing sign
and slide their secret
beneath a cairn.

Any given day a woman
on the street might be
two people.
The next day one of them
might be gone.
She might be glad,
gazing up at a peace sign
on the hill.

The city owns Waterworks.
Nobody remembers its first name.
You'd never know that people,
clasping shrunken placentas,
are buried up there.
Some of their secrets
killed them.
Some saved their lives.

There is no silence.
Hostage wind always
prods the hill,
sharpening its stones.
Bitterroots squeeze purple
from the ground, until
whole hillsides bleed.

The Baby within Her

will never be born. Its eyes
are dumb as marbles. It does not wail,

fawn inside a pickle jar
lifted from a dead mother.

All it wants is to hear her say No,
gentle and firm, and it will return

to the dark wool of the universe.
It will leave a blood trail:

frozen crystals like burgundy beads,
spilled mercury: tiny exclamations

or maybe tears
rolling on a slate of snow.

Good Friday

Two virgins unveil the clay body of Christ
on a cross and lift him up to be kissed.
His face is inscrutable but without pain,
no mark visible on his ribs.
My idolatry would be dishonest.
I don't join the holy queue.

The body of my grandmother was porcelain.
I knelt to kiss her forehead
and touch her elfin ears,
after she was dragged away
by one black leg,
the clot God's own finger.

She loved stray cats. Any flower.
Cakes, especially red velvet.
Her seven children. Me.
When she died I could not move.
The body operates via the mechanics of spirit.
Our sacrifice is to love.

I cannot take communion,
a thin wafer the priest offers, either.
I don't join the queue.
My grandmother's the one who died for me.
That mark is invisible.
I honor it.

Enduring Desire

What do I do with longing, silent and enormous
as a pair of bloody boots left by a door?
Longing is spirit separated from the body,
yearning to reunite. I'd like to box it up
and stick it on a shelf somewhere.

In fall's hoarfrost, a woman waited
in a cottonwood near a stream for elk.
When he came, she raised the rifle.
Even as the elk plunged to the ground,
something escaped out of the hole in his side
and went flying off through the forest.
Three days later, in her garage,
I saw the bull, still glorious, but cold,
rigid, one unforgiving eye staring up,
his spirit yet so close I could imagine
the clattering of his rack as he struggled to rise,
hooves skittering across concrete.
I could have knelt beside him,
stroking my sorrow into the wild ruse of his hide,
and apologized, since there's no turning back.

It was the longing to reassemble, or
this day to have my lover beside me again
in the church, while the Salish lift Christ's body
from the cross and parade it around twelve small fires.

Just outside town, a herd of fifty or more elk
lolls in the sunshine on the mountain.
The longing waits with them.

Day of the Dead

At dusk I join a parade in the town center:
gauze and poplin wraiths wobble through the streets.
The procession is a black army worm.
Along the way people set up altars
for recent grandmothers, irreplaceable lovers.
He's with me, among the candles, roses,
and old photographs—almost human and willing.
When the drumming starts, I dance, for hours.
I don't know how to be happy but I'm present
for a shower of meteors shattering the atmosphere,
a comet flaring in the western sky.
Early the next morning I walk past somnolent houses,
cold wreathing my neck, to visit
the statue of the Angel of Death.
Beyond empty benches, the angel waits,
most beautiful man ever known, copper skin
tarnished and streaked sharply with rain.
He has wings enough for us all.
Flowers have frozen in the ice at his feet.
I step so close he could draw his bronze wings
about me, and I look up into his eyes.
He is everything I ever wanted.
I'm here, I say.
Not yet, he tries to tell me.
Therefore I am reborn.
I can return to lilacs outside the kitchen window,
white enamel of table, cup of wisping tea,
a face I'll never see.

Carpe Momentum

In the deep rain of lilacs,
summer waits
with its brief berries,
grass, and corn sun.
How much sweeter
is the thing for which
we wait, hesitant,
knowing impermanence.
Once my lover
said to me, "We've
been waiting a long time
for this," before he
killed himself.
Summer approaches.
When it arrives,
I want to hold it hard,
no end in mind.

Loving a Dead Man

It is a cut forest.
Most of what was there is gone.
The rest functions as if nothing happened.
White violets bloom in low places
in the absence of every living tree.
Where the water tables, the ground leaks.
He was more oak than anything,
how it tends to splinter, and few of words.
I did not know the forest well enough,
relying instead on a traitorous calm:
I never walked it at night, for example,
when brown bats rested in sepulchral hollows
and the comet that slashes the sky
every thousand years flared above it all.
Two Western tanagers landed in firs overhead.
Resin oozed from hatches
in the bark of a Ponderosa pine.
He wanted to paint with it.
What he wanted now rots into the ground,
among skidder marks and discarded limbs.
Were it not for stumps, I would not know
a forest had been there.
Even after it grows back,
I'll be searching for clues.

Crucifix

Keep your eyes open.
Stay quiet.
Any moment now a speckled bird
will fly into the resurrection fern.
You must be ready
for that kind of deliverance.

V.

Earth, Our Lodging-Place

Not a day passes I don't consider catastrophe,
fires in Florida, no rain since February, days
too hot, smell of diesel, oil tanker overturned
in West River, trapping Eduard Stripling.
Our consolation was that hospice for the earth
would not be needed. No matter what, she would heal.
On the first day of June I find myself painting a room
for a small child I've never met who is dying, new brain
falling apart, sight going to white walls. Outside,
the wind rushes around as if unleashed,
looking for something to shake—branches, then
whole trees. The first drops are warning.
Something is upon us, with a sudden battery of thunder,
followed by an angry torrent.
The world trembles, shakes, heaves.
Hail pelts the windows like a seizure.
Arrows of lightning, a brilliant and holy fire,
shoot through the poignant house.
Is there no other way to redeem ourselves?

Mr. Coal

He don't care I was born in a house
used to stand back there, orchard was here,
over there now entirely gone was a stream
along which beech trees dropped their nuts,
our hogs fed on them.
Watch out for Mr. Coal, home-stealer,
tree-stealer, he don't care
who saved & built & planted.
He steals the pretty pink color
in your lungs, he steals the map
in your heart that shows you
how to get back.
Dirty thief.
Steals your neighbors, some sell out,
some go down to him, some like money,
green leaves wagging in their hands,
some go to work for him & think, think, think
they're doing the world a favor—
You like to burn your lights,
don't you? & they quit waving.
Friend of Mr. Coal no friend of mind.
I done heard too much about the man &
too many disappearances—
my daddy, my brother, my neighbor.
We are a remnant people in these hollers,
five hundred miles of streams
we played in buried,
rocky mountain creeks, springs &
clear sand bottoms, gone.
Tell me why my wellwater has turned
orange, why it smells,
why black specks float in it?
Mr. Coal sent papers, says mining is
to begin a halfmile from the house,

do we want a pre-blasting survey?
In case the old house tears
pillar from post.
He sends machines with tires taller
than the ceiling, he sends bull
dozers & a fleet of open
mouthed hauling trucks, tells the machines,
fall to eating.
They ate the mountain above the house,
the next mountain & the next.
I have lived in these parts all my life,
have seen them covered
with ice & snow & mist, bright yellow.
Like now. Not to mention
everything green. Plenty of flowers.
My god, every morning I woke & looked out,
glad to be alive in these old hills.
There's a map drawn here inside
& it looks like Breathitt County, Kentucky.
Right where the blood comes in is where
Massey tore down the mountain.
Mr. Coal, he lives down there under
ground. Wants to pull us all down with him:
Your people are all sick, what
you got to live for? he asks.
Down here, we can make us a bright light,
come on down.
He says this with his face dirty,
his teeth black, little halfmoons
under his fingernails pitch black.
His tongue is black.
His heart is darkest of all, nothing but a lump.
Mr. Coal carries around a rock
like the rest of us carry memories
until the overburden hits us
& they vanish too.

At the Livestock Sale

A man in the bleachers
told me he once killed a black bear,
heap of dark rags,
two of the legs like legs
and two like arms.
Another time he shot
five alligators in one afternoon.
At that I quit listening.
Did he shoot the gators
as they floated the black mirror
of some swamp pond,
breathing easily, dark and intriguing
eyes watching from the level?
Did they lift without will,
grotesque and unnatural,
into brilliant light?
Did he consume the flesh?
Or did he walk away from them
as from any common muskrat or mink
through whose brain
any one ever put a bullet?
Does he care that we're taking
the big woods down
to nothing, strips and edges?
Does he miss that bigness so desperately
he'll take whatever is left?
Or does he somewhere in his
violent outlaw heart feel
shambles of remorse?

Lost and Found

The people she worked for
when she first went to California,
Sylvia told me, had a kitchen
as big as my house, everything
enormous, granite
countertops four inches thick.
They slept on two king-sized beds.
They had a special bedcover
so heavy Sylvia couldn't lift it.
Their children each had a king-
sized bed. My son now almost grown
has slept since he was two on
a stained cotton futon. My husband
and I stick with our double.
The man of the house told Sylvia
he once made a commercial enemy,
vowed to put the man out
of business, which he did.
The man lost everything then his wife
left, and he killed himself.
That's horrible, Sylvia said.
He deserved it, the man said.
When he grew tired of lawn
furniture imported from Japan
he burned it, wouldn't donate
to the thrift stores, would rather
throw it away than let dirtballs
have something he worked hard for.
Oh, I shop there,
Sylvia said.
I'm not a dirtball.
Not you, the man said.

Twelfth Hour Lasts an Eternity

An iron chain slides its notes down a steel gate
keeping cows in Annick's meadow, music natural
as bluebirds or coyotes, familiar from days
spent at the end of Bear Creek Road.
Along the road, down the highway,
the miles to town, new houses are going up.
What was space, sky, mountain's green face,
is now roof, garage, dogyard, satellite dish.
Annick thought winter with its icy skids toward
the deathtrap of river and goddamned relentless cold
would scare people off, and it did. For a while.
Explain: why in one lifetime
must we watch the world disappear?
The mountains behind the ranch, miles deep, spiral
with logging roads as if pilgrims on some quest climbed,
and at the top, made the wrong prayers.
Annick climbs, praying. Even the Christ
could not hope for such a miracle.
At the edge of the meadow (summer-thick with fescue,
bunchgrass, shooting stars) something
lurks, peeping into Annick's log home.
The more crowded the valley, the harder
the thing pants. Nothing has struck it down.
Annick knows it's at the edge, waiting.
To move so much as an anvil
might tip the cliffs standing round (cloaked in trees)
and allow the enemy entrance. The chain is
(now, in my hands) a gong, striking iron.

Rant, WonderFarm

From a distance the heads of elderberries look like egrets
floating on the prison pond where cattle come to drink,
    or did,
before the Riverkeeper visited once,
                twice,

this dammed blackwater into which 10,000 acres of prison-farm
    drain:
acres that feed prisoners across the state,
charged with glyphosate aka Roundup,
    which the World Health Organization now calls
    "a probable carcinogen"
    which we know can last 40 years in the soil
    and which we have also come to understand is associated
        with Parkinson's
        with Alzheimers
        with autism
        autoimmune diseases in whose traces we take to our beds.

And these acres no different
        than our fathers' farms
        than our neighbors' farms
        than the 10,000-acre Roundup-Ready corn & cotton &
        soybean & canola
        more toxic by the day.

But on some land down the road
    where a sign says PLEASE NO SPRAYING
    where the kids are calling themselves *farmers*
        without the combines
        without subsidies—terrible erosion—chemicals—
    where bees are buzzing
    where buckeyes bloom in March when hummingbirds

have always returned to south Georgia
although no one can count on that now,

everything changing,
before our eyes changing.
    where cows rotate through the green pastures,
    kept out of the creek,
    where goats browse upward in the brush, the sheep graze.
Not one farmstead but many, Joe in his garden and Charlotte in
    hers,
Julia, Jamila, Rashid, Relinda in their gardens,
Joel in his fields and Wendell in his pastures,
Vandana in her seed bank.

They are not planting their grandfather's corn,
wholly place-adapted, vintage, heirloom, Mom & Pop corn.
    That's gone.
        But Stanley corn, Keener corn, Bloody Butcher corn.

Planting Candyroaster squash, Greenpeace kale,
    Mortgage Lifter tomato, Gold-striped cushaw,
    Green Glaze collards, Malabar spinach.

Planting cowpeas—Red Hull Javie, Colossus, Hercules, Blue
    Goose, Running Conch, Lady, Zipper Cream, Pinkeye Purple-
    hull.

Grounded again.

Picking the elder flowers that taste so good in pancakes and later
    the berries themselves, for syrup, wine, tincture.
Picking the ramps, the wild onion, sassafras, chickweed,
    lamb's-quarters, walnut.

Picking the chanterelles.
    With the books open,
    eyes wide open,
    hearts open, yes?
Speaking a new language:
    mizuna… Flemish Giant… fermentation… vermiculture…
    open-pollinated… raw… organic… local.

They ask the old guy who visits if he's ever had cracklins.
No, he says, but I know they're cooked in lard.
Has he ever tasted collard kraut? Clabber? Moon & Stars?
No, he says. No, no.

Food destroying us.
Nutritionally impotent.
Harming the earth.
Annihilating pollinators.

We have allowed industry to feed us.

But green is the new black,
the backyard the hottest vacation spot.
The holes in the atmosphere & those in our brains can heal.
Also the holes in our hearts.
People who shop at farmers markets are happier, happiest.
The farmer—neighbor, friend.

Everything changing,
before our eyes changing.

We're building soil now,
finally building soil:
local soil. Organic soil. Soul soil.

Building local energy, local power, local culture, local means.
Building community—look at us, all of us—

Taking the power back—
    political power
    power of place
    power of the sun
    nutritional power
    power of people to feed themselves
    power of deliciousness
    power of beauty....
Reclaiming
    hope
    vanishing genetics
    old wisdom and new
    the artistry of farming
    and the nourishment of art.

You ask will organics feed the world?
Will organics heal the world?
And I say,
    again,
        as always,
            Nothing. Else. Will.

I say, Rev up your awesome.
You. Find a place to push.
Pick up a tool, a hoe or a shovel.
Start turning the compost bin,
to make the soil in which
the seed will grow.

Make art.
Live art.
Farm art.
Go home.
Come home.
Savor.

We are winging into the Ecozoic,
everything changing,
before our eyes changing.

Welcome to the new world.

Trees

We live among trees,
sleep under them,
pass by and through them,
yet we mostly do not see them.
Mostly we are oblivious.

They shade us, shelter us, envelop us, moisten us.
They give us oxygen. All day and all night,
day after day, night after night,
they breathe for us.

They stand peacefully around us, allowing
birds and squirrels, bobcats and snakes inside them.
They sacrifice themselves to become our homes,
our art, our utensils, our furniture.
Turned into paper, they bear our words.
In cold weather they give themselves to keep us warm.
They become ghost trees, memory trees.

They feed us, offering their seeds, their nuts, their fruit,
their pomes, their leaves. They feed the animals we love.
They annoy us, dropping leaves, needles, cones and branches.
They make messes like children, we say.

They protect us from storms.
They protect us from each other.
They shield us, hide us, hold us,
as they shield, hide, and hold all kinds of life.
They make music for us—percussions, rattles, shivers.
They are wind instruments.
They sough, they weep, they wail and moan,
they sing. They call our names. They creak.
Mostly we don't hear them.
They exist beyond us.

Yet they are everything to us.
Without them we could not last. We could not be.
We are nothing without them.

And every day we destroy them.
We cut them, burn them, run over them,
scar them, skin them.
They sprout again.
They throw seeds and reproduce.
They coppice.

They never give up.
They never give up on us.
They never give up trying to save us.

Sicklefin Redhorse

From the lower reaches of Burningtown,
from Iotla and Forney, Deep and Hanging Dog,
they are a school of red horses
galloping up the mountain streams.
For thousands of years they have plunged upward
toward the future, and still they push
against swift waters, centuries eroding behind,
loss crashing and breaking over.
I will not stand in sorrow as long
as they need me to stand.
I will climb onto the bridge at Reliance
and watch them as they pass,
taste of dried fish bones like granite flakes,
Junigihtla, silt in the mouth,
red feathers dancing, horse beneath me,
pot of heavy bones.
I am carried away.
Yes, my brother too is dead.
Yes, when we gather before a fire
our house is divided, eroded, small.
Is there a list where I can write
my feast of casualties, as we chase the ages
into a stone weir and gather them?
My baskets are heavy with stones,
and the rock is coppery, brassy.
It glints and leaps, tails flying.
The rock fills my eyes, mouth, belly.
And yet they come, tumbling through
rushing waters, smoothing the edges of time,
out of the Tuckaseegee, the Hiawassee,
and the Oconoluftee, a herd of stones
spilling into the deep pools of their breeding,
so many the red feathers

make the rivers burn, fire-water, boiling stew.
I see the floating lilies of their eggs,
diaphanous veils and mists, the sacred female,
stallions waiting with the gilt of seed.
Because the first responsibility of the son
and the daughter is to return.
I see the ancestors coming down
with their baskets, the girls laughing on the
silver-wet boulders, the boys thigh-deep
in the rushing cold waters wrestling the wild red horses
the way boys will do. Corrals full of stones.
Streams of tears. Years eroding from the old mountains.
Their words filling my ears:
amaganugogv, soquili, aninvya.
I see my brother fishing from the thickets of rhododendron.
I see my grandmother next to him.
I see my uncles, my aunts, my father's cousins,
fishing for stone beside baskets of silt and dust
as the world crumbles to pieces.
Junigihtla, junigihtla, junigihtla: thundering
up the Nantahala, up Keener, from the impoundment at Fontana,
from the dam at Chilhowee, at Kagley, at Hensley Lake,
from below Sylva now that Dillsboro is down.
I see them leaping the dam at Ela.
The old people are laughing, white threads of fires
rising behind them, town feast, feast of love,
feast of stone. Soon the dancing will begin.

Janisse Ray is an American author whose work often grapples with the beauty, intricacy, and heartbreak of the biosphere. *Red Lanterns* is her second book of eco-poetry. She has published five books of literary nonfiction, including the acclaimed *Ecology of a Cracker Childhood* and *The Seed Underground*. Ray lives and works in coastal Georgia.

CPSIA information can be obtained
at www.ICGtesting.com
Printed in the USA
JSHW042256210421
13801JS00004B/15